WarNurses

WarNurses

by Shaaron Cosner

 WALKER AND COMPANY

NEW YORK

Photo credits:
Photos courtesy of the American Red Cross: frontispiece,
pp. 7, 19, 30, 37, 38, 43, 48–49, 55
Photos courtesy of the Armed Forces Institute of Pathology:
pp. 3, 14, 34
Photo courtesy of the National Archives: p. 25
Photos courtesy of the U.S. Army Center of Military
History: pp. 31, 40, 45, 47, 58, 60, 68, 77, 82, 86, 90
(bottom)
Photos courtesy of the Naval Photographic Center: pp. 72,
74, 75, 79, 81, 90 (top), 91

First published in the United States of America in 1988 by the Walker
Publishing Company, Inc.
Published simultaneously in Canada by Thomas Allen and Son,
Canada, Limited, Markham, Ontario.

Library of Congress Cataloging-in-Publication Data

Cosner, Shaaron.
    War nurses / Shaaron Cosner.
        p.   cm.
    Summary: Traces the history of organized military nursing during wartime,
from its beginnings during the Civil War to the recent conflict in Vietnam.
    ISBN 0-8027-6826-1. ISBN 0-8027-6828-8 (lib. bdg.)
    1. Military nursing—History—Juvenile literature. 2. Military
nursing—United States—History—Juvenile literature. [1. Military
nursing—History.] I. Title.
UH490.C67   1988   355.3′45—dc19   88-14245

Printed in the United States of America

10 9 8 7 6 5 4 3 2 1

Book design by Sylvia Frezzolini

To all nurses everywhere, especially Mary Ann,
who fought her own kind of war.

Contents

War Nurses

CHAPTER ONE

"...Sight-seers, do-nothings, idlers, time-killers, fops, and butterflies..."

It was three o'clock on an August morning in 1862. The bloody battle of Chantilly had just taken place the day before in thunderstorms so loud that the battle couldn't be heard three miles away in Centerville. A surgeon was now picking his way across the wet leaves, through the wounded and dead men that lay scattered about. His candle flickered like a weaving firefly as he made his way toward one lone woman seated on a box.

"Can you help me?" he asked.

Clara Barton nodded and followed him to where a young boy lay mortally wounded.

"Mary!" he cried.

Clara looked at the surgeon.

"His sister," he explained.

Clara motioned the surgeon away and knelt down. She placed her hand on the boy's neck, kissed his forehead, and laid her cheek against his.

"Mary," the boy said, gazing into her face. "You've come."

He ran his bloody hands over her face and entwined them in her tumbled hair. Clara wrapped the boy in blankets, gave him a drink of water, and prepared to care for him throughout the night while the doctor tended to others.

The next day the boy discovered his mistake, but he was very grateful.

"Put me on a train," he whispered. "I want my mother to get my body. Don't leave me to be buried in the woods."

The boy was placed on a train for home the next day and lived long enough to see his mother and his sister, Mary, before he died. Clara Barton, Civil War nurse, had relieved another boy's suffering.

When the Civil War began in 1861, it was only a matter of a few months before there were thousands of sick and wounded soldiers from both sides. They were packed into cattle cars to be taken to temporary hospitals in hotels, churches, schools, factories, warehouses, private homes, barns, prisons, tents, taverns—any place from a pigsty to the Rotunda of the U.S. Capitol.

In these overcrowded "hospitals" the patients were placed wherever there was room—on the damp ground, on planks of wood, or on rotten straw. They were lucky if someone gave them clean pine boughs or corn husks to rest on.

There were very few doctors during the Civil War and they were exhausted from trying to take care of so many patients. The patients were left to lie in the sun or rain for hours. They were bitten by mosquitoes and creeping insects. Pneumonia and dysentery, a kind of diarrhea, were common. For every two who died of wounds, five died of disease. The men knew their chances of surviving were better

2

Field hospital at Fredericksburg, Virginia, 1864

on the battlefield than they were in the hospitals. They would not go unless it was absolutely necessary.

The fact that the doctor would ask Clara to care for the wounded boy was the highest kind of compliment during the 1800s. At that time, a woman's place was in the home. Unmarried women were never left alone without a chaperone and they never cared for male patients unless they were members of their immediate families. The thought of a woman going into a battlefield or hospital to care for the diseased, wounded, and dying was unthinkable. A patient might be cared for by a friend or convalescent soldier, another patient who was getting well, but women were not welcome.

Women, however, had ignored what people thought and took care of the sick and wounded anyway. Back in the Revolutionary War, Roman Catholic nuns and Protestant sisters had taken care of the

Head-Quarters King's Division,

Aug 4 1862.

PASS Miss Barton

to Fredericksburg

and return.

BY ORDER GEN. KING:

Pass allowing Clara Barton to search for soldiers missing in action

wounded, and sometimes mothers, sisters, and wives insisted on following their loved ones to the battlefield to care for them. General George Washington had been one of the first to realize that nurses were needed. He offered a salary of "one fifteenth of a dollar per day or two dollars a month" to anyone who would become a nurse. Before he could bring in nurses, however, the war ended.

When the Civil War began, the only women still nursing male patients were from the religious orders. On December 26, 1862, four sisters of the Order of the Holy Cross boarded the *Red Rover,* a steamer that was being outfitted as a floating hospital for Confederate soldiers. These sisters were the first female nurses carried aboard a wartime hospital ship.

The doctors still resisted the thought of women in the hospitals. They said women would gossip too much and spoil the patients. They felt they were not disciplined enough for army life and were "useless annoyances." They said the women could not perform the simplest hospital chores like emptying a bed pan or turning a patient over, much less take care of horrible wounds and infections. One man called them "sight-seers, do-nothings, idlers, time-killers, fops, and butterflies."

Hundreds of women disagreed with this description and were so desperate to help that they disguised themselves as men. One of these, Mary Elizabeth Walker, was a doctor. Some, like Sarah Emma Edmonds, were nurses. Sarah called herself Franklin Thompson and served for two years as a soldier, spy, and nurse. When she contracted malaria in 1863, she deserted rather than go to the hospital where they would find out she was a woman.

Some women were allowed in hospitals simply because they demanded it. Mary Ann Bickerdyke was such a woman. Described as a large, heavy woman with "muscles of iron, nerves of finest steel,"

Mary Ann was a housewife in her forties from Galesburg, Illinois, when the war broke out. She went to the nearest hospital and began helping out as well as she could. One day a surgeon said to her, "There is no room for you in this hospital."

"I am staying," she said firmly. "And if you put me out one door I shall come in another. If you bar the door, I will come in the window. In fact, if anyone leaves, it will be you!"

On April 14, 1861, President Lincoln requested seventy-five thousand volunteers to help win the war. On August 25, 1861, the Women's Central Association of Relief was formed to prepare nurses for war by training them in New York hospitals, with Dorothea Dix, a woman famous for her work in what were then called insane asylums, as superintendent.

Georgeanna Woolsey wanted to be one of those nurses, but she was only twenty-eight years old, and regulations said prospective nurses had to be thirty. Dix wanted her nurses to be plain-looking women who wore gray, brown, or black dresses. She did not like hoops, bows, curls, or jewelry. Georgeanna lied about her age, took the flowers off her bonnet and the ruffles off her dress, and became a nurse. She was sent on the train to a New York hospital. There she was given two gray skirts and a short jacket similar to those worn by some soldiers. She also received four white aprons with large pockets, a washable petticoat, and a flannel dressing gown "to put on in a hurry and fly out if the city is bombarded or anything else." For street wear she was given a black dress and a black straw bonnet. She also got towels, old sheets, soap, cologne, sponges, small stoves, and a lamp. Her pay for scrubbing hospital floors and supervising the laundry was twelve dollars a month.

Like many others, Georgeanna Woolsey found that her services were often not welcome in the New York hospital. Once, while she

Civil War nurses in uniform

was fanning a dying man, a "Bogie," as she called the doctors, came by and told her she couldn't stay. She firmly informed him that she had ordered her carriage to return later in the day, the sun was hot, and she had no intention of walking out in it. In short, she was there for the day. She stayed not only that day, but many days after, doing what she could for the men.

Cornelia Hancock, a Quaker from New Jersey, also wanted to be a nurse. She traveled to Baltimore to meet Dorothea Dix. Miss Dix went down the line of young women who wanted to be nurses and chose them all except for Miss Hancock. She said Cornelia was too young and her cheeks were too rosy. Cornelia refused to be rejected, however. She got on board the train and defied Miss Dix and the train officials to take her off. When she arrived at Gettysburg with the other nurses, they needed help so badly they were happy to get Cornelia and anyone else who could help, whether Miss Dix had chosen them or not.

Clara Barton was another who found her services in demand once she reached the battlefield. Clara had been interested in nursing since she was eleven years old and had tended her brother for two years after he fell off a barn. At eighteen, Clara became a teacher, a career that lasted for fifteen years. During that time, she had several proposals of marriage, but she preferred to be independent. In 1854, at age thirty-three, she gave up teaching to become one of the first women to work in government. She became a clerk in the Patent Office in Washington. When the Civil War began in 1861, she went to Union Army officials and asked to be allowed to help at the battlefields. Despite opposition from the men in charge, she was eventually allowed to set out with a mule team loaded with medical supplies for the wounded and dying. Her experiences resulted in world fame and the title of "Angel of the Battlefield."

CHAPTER TWO

"Don't send your sweetheart a love letter. Send him an onion."

Not all women were as dedicated as Mary Ann Bickerdyke or Clara Barton. Many looked on war as an adventure and, horrified by what they saw when they arrived at the hospitals and battlefields, quit immediately. Others were as horrified but stayed.

Louisa May Alcott, author of *Little Women,* was one of those who thought nursing would be "fun." When she was selected as a nurse, she was most concerned with what she would wear. She wrote:

> As boys going to sea immediately become nautical in speech, walk as if they already had their "sea legs" on, and shiver their timbers on all possible occasions, so I turned military at once, called my dinner my rations, saluted all newcomers, and ordered a dress parade that very afternoon. Having reviewed every rag I possessed, I detailed some for picket duty while airing over the fence; some to the sanitary influences of the washtub; others to mount guard in the trunk; while

the weak and wounded went to the Work-basket Hospital, to be made ready for active service again.

When Louisa arrived at her new station, however, she found that war was certainly not fun. She began on New Year's Day, 1863, surrounded by hundreds of suffering men. Pneumonia, diphtheria, and typhoid were running rampant. The wounded and dying lay on muddy, bloody blankets, waiting for care. She wrote:

> The first thing I met was a regiment of the vilest odors that ever assaulted the human nose, and took it by storm. Cologne, with its seven and seventy evil savors, was a posy-bed to it; and the worst of this affliction was every one had assured me that it was a chronic weakness of all hospitals, and I must bear it.

Louisa began carrying a bottle filled with lavender water with her and became known as "the nurse with the bottle."

When Mary Ann Bickerdyke arrived in Cairo, Illinois, she found ten men crowded in each tent, sleeping on straw pallets and army blankets spread out on mud floors. Swarms of bluebottle flies were so loud she could hardly hear the moans of the suffering patients. The sick men were filthy; many were clad only in shirts or underwear.

Mary Ann Bickerdyke went right to work. She found a group of men around a campfire and, promising them a home-cooked meal, urged them to help her. Water was set to boil in every container. She gathered up cakes of strong brown laundry soap she had brought along and marched into the first tent. Using more bribes of food, she lured those who could walk to the tubs for a bath. She and her helpers cut all the patients' hair and whiskers off to get rid of the lice in them. She burned all their clothes, straw, and blankets. She gave the patients fresh clothes. She and her helpers shoveled the filthy mud out and laid down fresh straw and clean sheets. Then she began to prepare her home-cooked meal. No wonder she soon became known as the "Cyclone in Calico"!

When the nurses were in training, they had been told their duties would be to read to the patients, write letters, and do the housework. When they got to the battlefields they found themselves holding dying men, taking care of terrible wounds, and sometimes even performing emergency surgery.

Once Clara Barton was hard at work at Fredricksburg, Virginia, when one of the officers told her a man had been shot in the face and was in danger of suffocating from his own blood. She seized a basin of water and a sponge and ran to the church where he lay. When she began washing away the blood, she recognized him as a man from her own hometown.

Another time, at Antietam, Clara found a wounded man with a bullet lodged in his right cheek. He begged her to take it out. She opened the blade of her pocket knife, and while another wounded man held the patient's head, Clara took the bullet out and calmly washed and bandaged the man's face.

Sometimes the nurses were the only women present among thousands of men. When Mary Ann Bickerdyke arrived after the battle of Chattanooga, she was the only woman at the field hospital for nearly six weeks. At one time she had almost two thousand men to take care of.

Clara Barton was once described as the only woman "among that moving sea of men." When a general said he was afraid she was in danger, she told him she was probably the best protected woman in the United States. The soldiers listening nearby yelled, "That's so. That's so." Clara was allowed to stay.

Friends and family back home also worried about the nurses on the battlefields. They begged them to give up living in such squalid conditions in such dangerous areas. After working for five days and nights with only three hours' sleep and barely avoiding capture by enemy troops, Clara Barton wrote home:

> . . . if you chance to feel that the positions I occupied were rough and unseemly for a woman—I can only reply that they were rough and unseemly for men. But under all, lay the life of the nation. I had inherited the rich blessing of health and strength of constitution— such as are seldom given to women—and I felt some return was due from me and I ought to be there.

Most of the women had led very sheltered lives before they went to war, and some were quite young. But they soon got used to the terrible conditions they found. Seventeen-year-old Annie Etheridge of Detroit, Michigan, for instance, served as an Army nurse during the Civil War without pay. Troops called her "Gentle Anne," yet she participated in twenty-eight engagements and had two horses killed from under her. For her "noble sacrifice and heroic service" to the Union Army she received the Kearny Cross of Valor—one of the Union's highest battle decorations.

Susie King Taylor was a fourteen-year-old black girl living in Georgia when the Civil War began. She and her parents had escaped to a refugee camp for people who had lost their homes, and when Union officers found she could read and write, they put her in charge of a school of thirty children during the day and a class of adults at night. Eventually, she found herself performing nursing chores as well. She brought water and books to the wounded, straightened their beds, and washed their faces. When the dreaded disease small-pox broke out in the camp, the victims were isolated. But one of the men was from Susie's company, so she was allowed to visit him. When the surgeon found out that she was willing to risk her life, he made Susie a fulltime nurse, and she spent the rest of the war caring for the men. She wrote:

> It seems strange how our hatred to seeing suffering is overcome in war—how we are able to see the sickening sights, such as men with their limbs blown off, mangled by the deadly shells, without a shudder; and instead of turning away, how we hurry to assist in (easing) their pain, bind up their wounds and press cold water to parched lips, with feelings only of sympathy and pity.

Because of such intense feelings, the women often became very protective toward their patients. Once, Mary Ann Bickerdyke arrived at a hospital to find the patients unfed and uncared for. The surgeon in charge was drunk. She turned on him and shouted, "Here these men, any one of them worth a thousand of you, are suffered to starve and die all because you want to be off upon a drunk. Pull off your shoulder-straps, for you shall not stay in the Army a week longer."

Sure enough, the man was discharged, and when he appealed to General Sherman, he was told, "Oh, it's Mother Bickerdyke? Then I can do nothing for you. She outranks me."

While the women were at the battlefield, they often coped with the same conditions as the men. They sometimes had to live in tents or even sleep outdoors. While Clara Barton was at Petersburg, Virginia, she lived in a tent with a dirt floor "just like the street." She had a narrow bed of straw and a three-legged stand made of old cracker boxes.

Once Clara made her way back home, exhausted, only to find her

U. S. Sanitary Commission at General Hospital at Gettysburg, Pa.

tent floor covered with water. She chose a place where the water wasn't too deep and lay resting her head on her left arm so the water would not seep into her ears. She had been asleep for only two hours when she heard wagons arriving with more wounded.

"I sprang to my feet dripping wet," she said, "covered with ridges of dead grass and leaves, wrung the water from my hair and skirts, and went forth again to my work."

It was hard to find food during wartime for nurses and patients alike. If they were near a friendly town, they might be able to have food brought in. Then a nurse might have to oversee the distribution of gallons of coffee, dozens of eggs, barrels of applesauce, and hundreds of slices of buttered toast for breakfast. She might oversee the cooking of gallons of soup, barrels of potatoes, turnips, onions, or squash, gallons of pudding, and hundreds of apple pies for dinner.

When conditions were bad, everyone went without. In the field, there was no way to preserve the food, so the men had to make do with what was available in the area. If there was no food in the area, they did without. At Fredericksburg, Clara Barton saw men hold up "their cold, bloodless, dingy hands as I passed, and beg me in Heaven's name for a cracker to keep them from starving (and I had none); or to give them a cup that they might have something to drink water from, if they could get it (and I had no cup and could get none). . . ."

At the Second Battle of Bull Run, Miss Barton arrived with three other women to find they had two water buckets, five tin cups, one camp kettle, one stewpan, two lanterns, four bread knives, three plates, a two-quart tin dish, three thousand "guests" to serve—and no food.

At Antietam, Clara had cut her last loaf of bread and pounded her last crackers. All they had left were three boxes of wine.

"What should we do?" one of the helpers asked.

"Open the wine, distribute it and then 'God help us,' " Clara said.

They opened the three boxes and found that the wine had been packed in corn meal! It was enough to make a nice gruel for the men. Later, they decided to explore the cellar of the house where they were staying, and there they found another treasure—three barrels of flour and a bag of salt!

Milk and eggs were extremely hard to come by in the South. They couldn't be shipped because they would spoil, so local farmers knew they could charge outrageously high prices for inferior products, like the milk that Mary Ann Bickerdyke said was "two-thirds chalk and water." She told the commander that the milk was so bad, if it were put into the trough of a respectable pig at home, he would turn up his nose and run squealing off in disgust.

Another time, Mary Ann again went to bat for her "boys." She proposed to bring in fresh milk and eggs if the commander would give her a leave. She went home, rounded up one hundred cows, and had them shipped by train to Memphis in herds of twenty. Then she gathered up a bunch of chickens and had them sent. Mary Ann Bickerdyke's patients soon had their fresh eggs and milk.

In one area, a nurse named Mary Livermore, a friend of Mary Ann Bickerdyke's, plastered the villages with posters reading, "A barrel of potatoes for every soldier," or "Don't send your sweetheart a love letter. Send him an onion." They also promoted "Victory Gardens" around the army camps to provide their patients with fresh vegetables.

Because supplies were so scarce, the nurses carried everything they could with them. They could be seen with baskets filled not only with rice puddings, currant jellies, broiled salt codfish, molasses gingerbread, boiled custard, soda crackers, gum drops, and baked apples, but writing supplies, reading material, games, knives, sewing supplies, and music books.

Clara Barton tried to carry "every article ever thought of" with her. Once at Antietam she found a surgeon gazing at a little bit of candle he had left. He told her angrily that he had one thousand wounded, five hundred of whom would probably die before day-break because he didn't have light enough to care for them. Miss Barton took him to the door and pointed to a brightly lit barn nearby. She had brought four boxes of lanterns with her.

With supplies so limited, the nurses often became very possessive and jealously guarded what they had. When Mary Ann Bickerdyke saw a civilian wearing clothes that should have gone to a patient, she seized the culprit by the collar, undressed him before all the patients, and said, "Now, you rascal, let's see what you'll steal next."

When food began disappearing, Mrs. Bickerdyke bought tartar emetic, a mixture that makes people vomit. She mixed it with some freshly stewed peaches, and left them on a table "to cool" over night. Soon everyone could hear the moans and groans of the men who had been stealing the food. The men were arrested, and she locked the food box with a strong lock.

Lack of food and sleep, along with primitive sleeping quarters, meant the nurses often became sick themselves. Louisa May Alcott became deathly ill but refused to leave "her boys." Her father was forced to make a trip to take her home so her family could take care of her. Some nurses died because they refused to stop caring for their patients.

In addition to illness, the nurses were often in physical danger as well. During the battle of Fredericksburg, Clara Barton received a bloody, crumpled slip of paper from a surgeon requesting her help. She made her way across a swaying bridge with shells exploding all around her. One blew away part of her clothing and the arm of an officer who had rushed to help her. An instant later another officer was hit, and when Clara arrived at the hospital she learned he had died. Another time, at Antietam, she had just raised a man's head to give him a drink when a bullet flew between them, tore a hole in her sleeve, and killed the patient.

News of the nurses' brave deeds and courage reached the people back home and many of them became national heroines. Their pictures were hung in parlors and people wanted to give them receptions and parties when they came to town. They received all kinds of medals and honors, but most of them avoided the fuss and, during peacetime, settled down to working for better nursing conditions. In Clara Barton's case, her new mission was the founding of the American Red Cross.

After the Civil War, Clara spent years lobbying for the Geneva Convention, a treaty that would guarantee protection for the wounded. While traveling as a lobbyist in Europe, she heard about an organization called the Red Cross—an organization that helped people in times of disaster.

Clara served as a Red Cross volunteer at Strasbourg, France, during the Franco-Prussian War of 1870–71. When she returned to the United States, she began trying to convince people that America needed a Red Cross. At first they were skeptical. America would never go to war again. Why would they need a Red Cross? Clara pointed out that the Red Cross could help people in peacetime, during natural disasters. In 1881, she set up the first local Red Cross unit in Dansville, New York. That same year there was a huge forest fire in Michigan and Clara's Red Cross unit was there to help.

The publicity Clara was getting finally convinced President Chester Arthur that the Red Cross would really be helpful, and on May

Clara Barton founded the American Red Cross

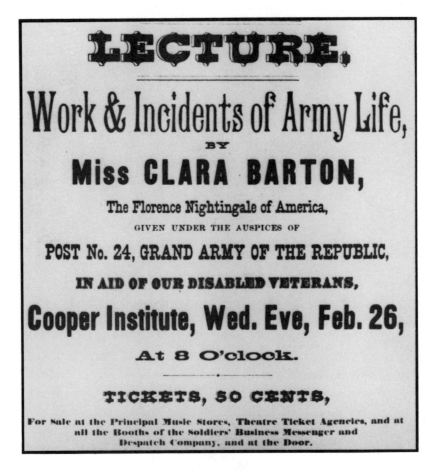

Poster Announcing Clara Barton Lecture

21, 1881, the American Red Cross became official. Clara was made president of the organization and became known as "the Queen" and "Our Lady of the Cross." She helped form Red Cross units across the United States. In the decade before the Spanish-American War, her organization aided many people in disasters such as the Mississippi flood of 1884, the Johnstown flood of 1889, and a devastating hurricane in Galveston in 1893.

CHAPTER THREE

"The Lady with the Lamp"

Seven years before the Civil War broke out in the United States, a young woman left her wealthy home in England for the Crimea, a large peninsula that juts out from the southern part of Russia. Florence Nightingale had been interested in helping the sick since she was a small child, much to the horror of her wealthy parents. At the age of seventeen, she wrote in her journal, "On February 7, 1837, God spoke to me and called me to His service." This, more than anything, convinced her she should serve mankind in some way.

Florence's family tried their best to interest her in what they considered more ladylike activities. They took her to dances and parties. They took her to Europe. She was presented to Queen Victoria. But Florence thought most of these activities were a waste of time. She quarreled constantly with her family, especially her mother, and the entire family was upset by her stubbornness.

In 1845, she approached her family with a plan to study nursing at a nearby hospital. Although they had finally agreed to let her care for family members and tenants on their lands, the thought of a Nightingale, especially a woman, working in a hospital was horrible!

"Only poor people who have nowhere to go enter the hospital," her mother shouted. "The hospitals are filthy, overcrowded, and filled with cockroaches and mice. Only women of the lowest rank work there. No. Absolutely not!"

Florence was devastated by their lack of understanding, but soon had her hopes raised again during a trip to Germany. In a small village called Kaiserswerth, she visited the local hospital and found it clean and well organized. The founder of the hospital, Theodore Fliedner, explained how he had begun a nursing school to train young women to care for the sick. It was a dream come true for Florence.

"May I train with you?" Florence asked.

The Reverend Fliedner was taken aback. He explained that the women training at his hospital were from nearby farms. Florence convinced him she could handle the hard work, and he finally agreed. Unfortunately, Florence's parents still refused to approve of her training in a hospital, not even one as clean and well run as the Reverend Fliedner's.

After much soul-searching, Florence finally knew that the only way she would ever be able to fulfill her goal of becoming a nurse would be to defy her parents. After many violent arguments, she left to train at Kaiserswerth in the summer of 1851. Her family secretly thought the hard work and long hours would send her hurrying back to the comfort of her home, but she wrote, "I find the deepest interest in everything here, and am so well in body and mind. This is life. Now I know what it is to live and to love life. . . . I wish for no other earth, no other world but this."

After her return to England, Florence became an expert on nursing and hospitals. In 1853, when the Crimean War broke out between Russia and the combined forces of England, France, Sardinia, and Turkey, Sidney Herbert, Britain's Secretary of War, decided to send Florence and a group of nurses to Scutari, a Turkish village near the Black Sea. He wrote, "There is but one person in England that I know of who would be capable of organizing and superintending such a scheme. . . . The difficulty of finding women equal to a task, after all, full of horrors, and requiring, besides knowledge and goodwill, great energy and great courage, will be great. . . ."

On October 21, 1854, Florence and thirty-eight nurses set sail for Scutari. When they arrived, they were appalled by conditions at the hospital. Nothing they had read in the British newspapers had prepared them for a hospital built over a huge cesspool, with wood so rotten it fell apart when scrubbed. Four miles of patients lay on the floor or on straw mattresses. Rats and insects scurried over the patients, some of whom lay half-naked in the bitter cold. The nurses were expected to live in six small rooms so cold their writing ink froze in the bottles. It was said the medical officer secretly hoped they would become discouraged and return to England.

Despite opposition from the doctors, the nurses went to work immediately. They made their tiny rooms as homey as possible. Florence had brought her own supplies for the patients and used her own money to send for more. Additional money came from a British newspaper fund, and over a period of months, Florence purchased fifty thousand shirts, thousands of knives, forks, towels, and socks, as well as many other basic necessities for her patients. Only six months later, the soldiers were well fed, clean, and clothed. The cesspool had been drained and disinfected, and deaths dropped dramatically.

Meanwhile, new patients poured into the hospital every day, and in December, Florence was told five hundred more would be coming. Desperately, Florence suggested that the army fix a burned-out wing of the hospital into wards for the expected men. The officers in charge refused. Florence got more money from the newspaper, but the workers she had hired went on strike and the newspaper withdrew its funds. Florence hired two hundred new workmen with her own money and restored the wing in time for the new patients.

Florence often spent sixteen to twenty hours working. She spent her days nursing the sick and wounded, and her nights taking care of administration of the hospital. She wrote letters to each family who had lost a son at Scutari that winter. She often worked and wrote until dawn. After a few hours of exhausted sleep, her day would begin again.

On December 14, 1855, Queen Victoria wrote to Florence and asked for advice on gifts to send to the soldiers. Florence wrote back suggesting the best gift she could give the soldiers was a new military pay system. She convinced the queen that it was unfair for men who were wounded in battle to be docked when they weren't able to fight anymore. On February 1, the pay scales were changed.

Florence became a heroine to the sick and wounded men of the Crimea that bitter winter of 1855. One man wrote, "What a comfort it was to see her pass even. She would speak to one and nod and smile to as many more; but she could not do it all, you know. We lay there by hundreds. But we could kiss her shadow as it fell, and lay our heads on the pillow again, content."

The soldier's description of Florence was published all over the world, and the American poet Henry Wadsworth Longfellow made her famous as "The Lady with the Lamp." Songs were written about

Florence Nightingale: "The Lady with the Lamp"

her, parents named their baby daughters Florence, statuettes were sold on the streets of London, and books and newspaper articles were written. The family that had once forbidden her to nurse the sick was now thrilled to have a celebrity.

Miss Nightingale saw two thousand men die that winter. She herself came down with "Crimean fever" while visiting a neighboring hospital in 1855, and was near death for two weeks. It was said when the news that she was sick reached her patients back at her hospital, the men turned their faces to the wall and wept. When Queen Victoria was informed that she had recovered from her illness, she set up a Nightingale Fund to establish a school for training nurses.

On March 30, 1856, a peace treaty was signed. Britain and her allies had won the war, and the last patient left Scutari on July 16. Florence returned home in August. She was supposed to have been welcomed by a parade, parties, and receptions, but she registered as "Miss Smith" on the ship and arrived home anonymously. She spurned all efforts of her countrymen and women to honor her. She was too busy reforming medical conditions in the British Army. She met with Queen Victoria and urged her to help. When she left, Queen Victoria exclaimed, "What a head! I wish we had her at the War Office!" A commission was organized and the procedures were changed. Because she was a woman, she was not allowed to take an active role in the commission, but did so indirectly, through Sidney Herbert, her old friend who had sent her to the Crimean War.

Florence spent the rest of her life writing books on nursing and setting up her school for nurses, which opened on July 9, 1860. Eventually, graduates of the Nightingale School were in great demand all over the world. Most of this work and writing was done from bed, because Florence had become an invalid.

For fifty years, Florence conducted business from her room. She consulted by mail with President Lincoln on organizing hospitals for the Union Army, and she corresponded with Dorothea Dix on giving proper care to patients.

In November, 1907, Florence Nightingale became the first woman to receive Great Britain's Order of Merit. Six years before, she had become blind, and so she, who had nursed so many others, was taken care of by relatives until her death on August 13, 1910, at the age of ninety.

CHAPTER FOUR

Our Lady of
the Cross

In 1898, U.S. President McKinley was trying to settle a dispute between Cuba and Spain. Cuba wanted to be an independent country; it did not want to be under Spanish rule anymore. Then the American warship *Maine* was blown up in Havana's harbor. It was never revealed who was responsible for the bombing, but public outrage forced the United States into a new war. "Remember the Maine" became the cry of those who fought the Spanish-American War. Admiral George Dewey rushed to the Philippines, also a Spanish-run country, and quickly defeated the Spaniards at Manila Bay. Heroic battles were also fought in Cuba during the Spanish-American War, and many men were wounded despite the fact that the conflict lasted only four months.

Doctors still believed nurses might be too independent and might demand unnecessary luxuries like bureaus, rocking chairs, and mirrors, and they wanted to keep nurses out of this war. Unfortunately, severe epidemics of typhoid and yellow fever in Cuba and the Philippines once more forced them to accept female help.

Dr. Carlos Finlay, a Cuban physician, believed yellow fever was transmitted by a certain type of mosquito. The U.S. Army asked for human volunteers to help him with tests. One of the volunteers was Clara Louise Maass, a graduate of the Newark German Hospital Training School for Nurses in New Jersey.

Clara Maass had cared for yellow fever victims in Manila, and in 1901 she arrived in Cuba for the experiments. In June, she allowed herself to be bitten by a mosquito and had a slight case of yellow fever. She wrote her mother saying, "Do not worry, mother, if you hear that I have yellow fever. Now is a good time of the year to catch it if one has to. Most of the cases are mild, and then I should be immune and not be afraid of the disease anymore."

The people conducting the experiments were not sure Clara's case had been strong enough, so she allowed herself to be bitten again. Ten days later she died.

Meanwhile, Clara Barton, founder of the American Red Cross, was now seventy-seven years old, but she was not to be excluded from this new war. When the Spanish-American War began, Clara Barton and other Red Cross nurses sailed from Key West, Florida, on June 20, 1898, with fourteen hundred tons of supplies. Their ship anchored off the coast of Cuba, at Guantánamo, a little town with no harbor and no docks. The women rowed to shore and went to work, often traveling from place to place in a hay wagon to deliver badly needed supplies.

One of the most famous army divisions, the Rough Riders, headed by Colonel Theodore Roosevelt, lost many of their supplies at the battle of San Juan. Roosevelt, who would later become president of the United States, offered to buy supplies from Miss Barton.

"They are not for sale at any price," she told him.

Nurses on their way to Cuba during the Spanish American War

"Leisure Hour at Camp" Spanish American War nurses, 7th Army Corps, Savannah, Georgia, 1898

"How can I get them?" the colonel asked.

"Just ask for them," Clara replied.

Eventually Clara ended up in the town of Santiago, where a Red Cross ship was docked. The ship had to wait for four days for mines to be removed so it, along with the rest of the American fleet, could enter. On the fourth day, Clara received the message that the Red Cross ship would be the first to enter.

"Could it be possible," Clara wrote, "that the commander who had captured a city declined to be the first to enter—that he would hold back his flagship and himself and send forward first a cargo of food on a plain ship, under the direction of a woman?"

After the United States defeated the Spanish, the nurses were stationed aboard the army transport, the *Lampasas,* with 102 patients taken from other crowded hospital ships. Conditions on board the ship were terrible. The nurses borrowed brooms from the sailors to sweep up the dirt. Ship fire pails were used to carry water; boxes served as tables and cupboards. Patients had only condensed milk and beef extract to eat, and nurses were kept busy brushing flies off the eyelids and throats of unconscious patients. They sometimes had to keep delirious men from jumping overboard.

Clara Barton had remained behind to work. When she finally returned to the United States she was criticized for leaving the country during time of war, especially for leaving others to carry out her duties at the Red Cross. Still, people could not ignore her courage and fortitude. She is remembered as one of the most outstanding women in American history.

CHAPTER FIVE

"...Patriotism is not enough."

When World War I started in Europe in 1914, the United States was at first not involved. Still, we did send nurses and hospital ships to Europe. In September, 1914, the *Red Cross,* also known as "The Mercy Ship," sailed for Europe. The huge white ship was decorated with a broad red stripe, with a red cross painted on its funnel. It flew the Red Cross and the American flags. Between September and December of the next year, over two hundred and fifty Red Cross nurses were sent to Europe; more than half sailed on "The Mercy Ship."

Navy nurses were sent to England, Ireland, and Scotland. Some were loaned to army field units in France. Schools of nursing were established in St. Croix and St. Thomas in the Virgin Islands.

In Europe, the American nurses wore uniforms of gray, with a white apron, white cap, and blue capes lined in scarlet. They traveled to some of the most exotic and primitive places in the world.

Field Hospital in France. 1918

Five nurses were sent to Khoi in Persia, seventy-five miles from the nearest railroad. They worked in an adobe building that had been used as an overnight stop for camel drivers. The local people loved to watch the nurses work and they had to get used to caring for their patients under curious eyes. When other towns asked for their help, they traveled in a camel caravan and camped in the desert.

In 1915 the passenger ship *Lusitania* was torpedoed by a German submarine. More than one thousand people lost their lives. America entered the war. One of the first casualties of World War I was a nurse named Edith Cavell. Edith was a British nurse serving in Belgium when the war started. Unaffected by the politics of war, she nursed any person who was wounded, even those who were German. She also helped a large number of Allied soldiers escape across the Belgian frontier into Holland or France after their wounds had healed. She protected young Belgians who did not want to go into the German military service by hiding them.

Eventually, the Germans discovered her activities and she was sentenced to death. Ambassadors of other nations appealed to Germany to let her go, but on the morning of October 11, 1915, she was taken to a garden, where a German officer took a pistol from his belt and shot her. She left behind a message that said: "Standing as I do in view of God and Eternity, I realize that Patriotism is not enough. I must have no hatred or bitterness towards anyone."

After Edith Cavell's death, many tributes were paid to her bravery. A mountain in the Canadian Rockies was named after her and a monument was erected in London to her memory.

Nurses of World War I had to face new problems and deal with new kinds of wounds. The Germans had advanced weapons like Big Bertha, a gun so huge it was pulled by thirty-six horses. It could shoot a 1,800-pound shell nine miles.

Aircraft were also being used for the first time in war, so patients involved in crashes were brought in. Poison gas was used in the trenches, so nurses had to treat skin burns, blindness, choking, and near-suffocation the gases caused.

The nurses also ran into certain social problems during World War I. They were not allowed to associate with officers or officers' wives. If they were captured, they lost their pay for as long as they were held captive. They were given enlisted men to help them in the hospitals, but the nurses were actually below privates in rank, so they had no real authority. Some of the orderlies were educated, well-to-do men who had been drafted. They had never taken orders from women before and resented the menial chores they were forced to do. This meant the cleaning, scrubbing, and emptying of wastes often went undone. If the nurses reported the men, they became even angrier.

Back in the United States, meanwhile, campaigns had begun to recruit tens of thousands of "subnurses," "housekeepers for the sick," and other volunteers who could be trained as quickly as possible. Three nurses in New York City, Lillian Wald, Annie W. Goodrich, and Adelaide Nutting, also worked to get better-qualified war volunteers into nursing schools. When the Army opened a School of Nursing, it got ten thousand applications. The army and navy also started reserve programs for emergencies, and about eighteen hundred black nurses were certified by the American Red Cross for duty with the military. However, these nurses were only sent to hospitals where there was a "colored cantonment," and since there were very few black units, their services were seldom utilized.

Nurses who trained for World War I studied anatomy and physiology, chemistry, bacteriology, hygiene, hospital housekeeping, nutrition, and the history of nursing. They participated in military

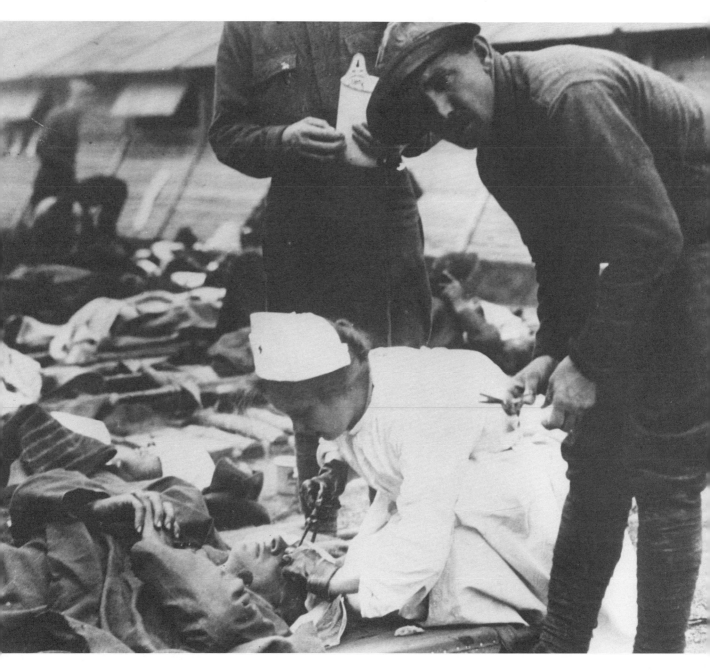

Red Cross nurse at field hospital in France during World War I bathes the eyes of a gassed soldier

Have you answered the Red Cross Christmas Roll Call?

American
Red Cross
poster

drills dressed like soldiers in trousers, army shoes, overcoats, and hats. They jumped ditches, climbed poles, and wriggled under barbed wire. They ate from tin plates at long, wooden tables. A social director at each camp saw to it that none of the women got involved in any romances. In fact, they were not even allowed to speak to men except to carry out their nursing chores.

The nurses were shipped overseas as quickly as they graduated. Many of them were sent to the front lines and worked in field hospitals that were often bombed. One nurse in France recalled five night raids in one week. Only about a fourth of the nurses had helmets to protect them, so they used water pails or wash tubs on their heads. Three nurses were wounded there and two were killed. Many others received medals for their bravery.

After their vigorous training in the States, some nurses, however, were surprised to find that their duties overseas were very different from what they had expected. Some were assigned to keep the fires going at all times in the messrooms. Some were assigned to transportation, driving ambulances in twenty-four-hour shifts and sleeping between assignments. They also found themselves cleaning engines or repairing and washing vehicles.

The food situation had hardly changed since Civil War days. Sometimes the only things they had to eat were chocolate and stale biscuits or hard bread and rancid margarine. Canteen food was so vile it sometimes made them sick. One nurse wrote, "We are always hungry in varying degrees—hungry, starving, or ravenous." She said, "The principal dinner dish is a sort of disgusting soup—stew made of meat that hangs over a drain until it is cut up—sinister looking joints of some strange animal—what we cannot decide."

In France, some of the nurses lived in huts with paper windows and mice scampering along the rafters. The wind blew down the stovepipes and put out the fires. Cotton was stuffed in the cracks in the ceilings and windows. Still, the snow drifted through, so that hands were often chapped and bleeding. The nurses wore bed socks on their heads and sometimes had as many as nine blankets on the bed in their efforts to keep warm.

It was a new experience also to have to cope with different languages and cultures in this war that involved many different countries. One nurse in a French hospital became known as "Arab

Julia Stimson, Chief of Army Norse Corps, being awarded Distinguished Service Medal by General Pershing. France, 1919

Mother" because of her ability to speak Arabic. One day she was called to attend an Arab who was giving the other nurses trouble.

"Arab Mother," the patient wailed, "they are oppressing me! I am a worm, scorned, tormented!"

The nurse asked what was wrong.

Finally, the patient sobbed out the whole terrible story. "My son of a hen was cooked too hard!"

"Such a fuss for one egg!" the nurse exclaimed.

More than twenty-three thousand American nurses served in the Armed Forces and the Red Cross during World War I. They received many honors for their work and were proud of their accomplishments. One nurse, Elizabeth Ashe, remembered that the nurses were asked by the French government to march in a parade. She said:

> I carried the flag; it was the proudest moment of my life. In fact, I don't think I ever had that proud feeling before. But when we fell in line behind the Marines, our band playing Dixie and I held that banner on high to the cheers of the crowd "Vive l'Amerique," I really felt that I had reached the supreme moment of my life.

CHAPTER SIX

"Holy Mackerel,
"An American Woman!

The hospital ship *Solace* lay slumbering among cruisers, destroyers, and battleships on Sunday, December 7, 1941. Americans stationed on the ship and on land at beautiful Pearl Harbor in Hawaii were just starting to get ready for church; some were sleeping in. The sound of airplanes flying overhead was not uncommon, but suddenly several planes went into a steep dive and began bombing the ships. People outside could clearly see the red suns painted on the wings. The planes were Japanese!

Nurses in the nearby barracks looked on in horror as the harbor suddenly became a mass of flames, smoke, and screams. After the initial shock, the nurses went into action. Beds were set up. Blood plasma bottles, drugs, and bandages were made ready, and the windows were quickly painted black so the Japanese would not be able to see the lights at night. A Japanese plane crashed in a hibiscus bush right by the hospital, but the women continued to race against time, for that night the wards would be filled with row after row of casualties.

Germany had invaded Poland in September 1939, and France and Great Britain had immediately declared war on Germany. During the following year, Germany swept into Norway, Denmark, Belgium, the Netherlands, and Luxembourg. France fell to the Germans in May, and the British feared they would be next. The British were

American Red Cross nurse with servicemen from Air Force, Army, Navy, and Marine Corps

also fighting the Italians in Africa. On the other side of the world, Japan had joined Germany and Italy. The United States had resisted entering the war, but now, with the bombing of Pearl Harbor, the Americans knew they would have to fight.

Nurses volunteered by the thousands and were quickly processed through long lines of inoculations (tetanus, typhoid, and typhus) and given supplies such as a musette bag or sack for carrying personal articles, gas masks, helmets, mess kits, canteen belts, and a bedroll consisting of a huge canvas mat with leather straps and pockets on each end.

Before they left the United States, they were trained more thoroughly than nurses had ever been trained before. They learned to make bed pans out of newspapers, stretchers out of trousers, and to sterilize, using ordinary items available. They learned to pitch tents and to camouflage themselves. Samples of dangerous gases were set off around them so they would be able to identify them under combat conditions. They learned how to put out incendiary bombs. The army set up a chamber that could be flooded with tear gas. The women were taught how to crawl through the chamber without being overcome by the tear gas. They practiced crawling across trenches and under barbed wire with machine gun fire all around them. They trained in the snows of Wisconsin and the deserts of California.

After World War I, nurses had fought hard to be awarded rank like their male counterparts. They entered World War II as second lieutenants. Still, a man could work his way up to general, but a nurse could go no higher than major in the army and lieutenant commander in the navy. Men sometimes earned twice as much money as the nurses even though many nurses had taken pay cuts from their civilian jobs to go to war.

44

Field Training, World War II

World War II nurses did enjoy most of the privileges offered other military personnel—post theaters, movies, swimming pools, free medical and dental care, and post exchange privileges allowing them to shop for everything from toothpaste to clothing. They could not be married, but could be divorced or widowed. They were not allowed to date enlisted men. Nurses in the armed forces were awarded a month's vacation and a month's sick leave, and could retire after twenty years of service with pay.

Army nurses were issued various uniforms suitable for a global war taking place from the Arctic to the tropics. On the bases, they wore olive drab uniforms. In field hospitals, they wore one-piece wrap-around uniforms of brown and white pin-stripe seersucker. This kind of material was easy to wash. (Wash-and-wear had not yet been invented.) The uniform's colors also faded easily into the background for camouflage.

In front-line war zones, the nurses wore trousers and shirts similar to the men's. They had shoes that laced up to the ankle, and leggings to protect them from marshes and mosquitoes. The trousers had "cargo pockets" to hold supplies. The nurses also wore standard army helmets.

In the Arctic, nurses' uniforms were the same as those worn by the ski troops—reversible parka, white on one side, khaki on the other, fur-trimmed hood, ski pants, and a close-fitting jacket. They also needed sturdy gloves and water-repellent shoes for the snow.

During World War I, Army nurses had been permitted to work only at evacuation hospitals, the last stop before the patients were sent home. In World War II, they were much closer to the fighting. During a battle, the wounded were first sent to front line hospitals located in tents close to the fighting. As soon as it was possible to move the patients, they were sent to the second stage of care, the

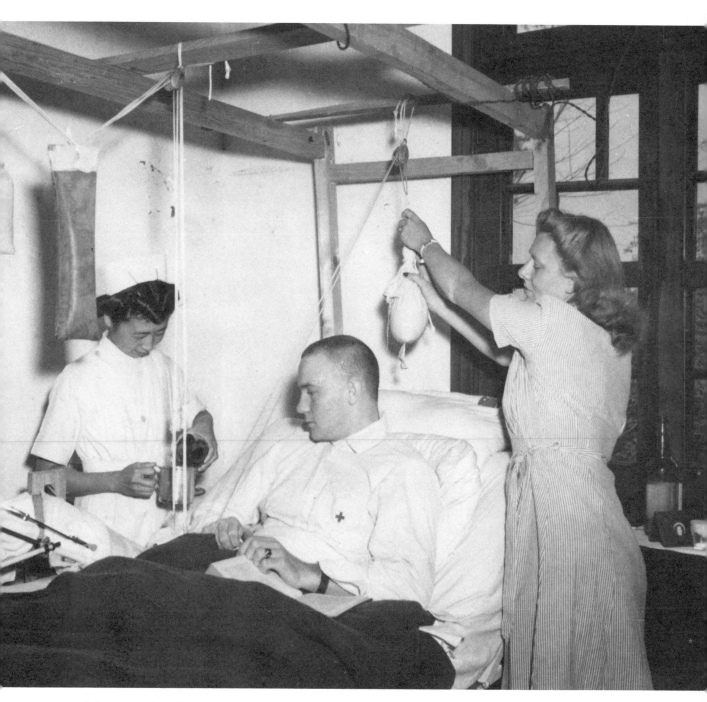

Nurses caring for patient in 95th Station Hospital, Kon-Ming, China. WWII.
1944

Red Cross hospital workers attached to combat unit in Italy in WWII

field hospitals located a little farther from the battle. From there they were moved to the evacuation hospitals for processing home. Nurses in World War II saw duty in all three types of hospitals.

Some of the nurses never saw the battlefields, for they served aboard transport planes that took the patients home from the war. This did not mean that their tour of duty was any less dangerous than those stationed on land or on shipboard. Thirteen American nurses were stationed aboard a transport plane that flew wounded from battlefields in Italy to the evacuation hospital in Cantania, Sicily. On the morning of November 8, 1943, the plane took off through a thin, gray mist on a return flight from Cantania. Halfway to their destination, they hit a storm. It was only a two-hour flight, but four hours later they had not reached their destination. They were lost.

Finally, the pilot saw an airfield below. He started to land, but at the last minute, pulled up sharply. The other planes on the airfield were German. They were behind enemy lines with little gas left in their tank. They were eventually forced to land in a cornfield in a driving rain. As the nurses, corpsmen, and crew of four piled off the plane, they saw gun-carrying men running from all directions. They thought they were in German hands, but the men turned out to be Albanian freedom-fighters who led them into the mountains, hiding them in cottages along the way. They slept on the floor among goats and sheep and existed on little food, since the Germans had taken most of the food the Albanians had.

At one point, the Albanians had hidden the Americans in a small village. Suddenly they heard a rumbling, and huge German tanks appeared in the street. The Americans and Albanians ran for the hills. When they stopped, they realized that three of the nurses were missing. There was nothing they could do. The Albanians got a message to the British Secret Service, and three transports, thirty-six fighter planes, and a bomber were sent to rescue them, but the Americans below couldn't make their location known because there were too many Germans in the area. All they could do was watch as the planes flew away. Finally they made their way through a blizzard, over the mountains. A 26-mile march brought them to the coast, where they were picked up by a British ship.

Meanwhile, the three nurses left behind, Wilma Lytle, Ann Maness, and Helen Porter, were still hiding in the village in a cellar. The Germans were camped right across the street. The Germans were sure there were Americans in the village, and often searched the houses two or three times. The house where the nurses were hidden had a secret tunnel leading to the house next door. When the Germans searched one house, the nurses simply made their way through the tunnel to the house next door. It was months before they finally escaped, dressed as peasants. They reached the coast and were rescued by the British on March 22, 1944.

The nurses of World War II found themselves stationed in areas all over the world. Some were sent to England, which had been besieged since the summer of 1940. There, civilian, armed forces, and Red Cross nurses worked frantically to keep up with the casualties streaming in after each German bombing. Homes and businesses were destroyed, and workers constantly pulled the wounded and dead from the debris. Each time the air raid sirens sounded, they signaled the beginning of more casualties.

Some of the nurses who left for the European front were stationed aboard hospital ships. The ships anchored off shore from battle areas and waited for the landing barges to make their way through choppy seas to the side of the white hospital ships. There, the spray-soaked wounded would be hoisted aboard. Soon the clean decks would be covered with blood. One soldier wrote, "The ship smelled of blood, vomit, corruption, and hot feverish flesh." Yet, he added, he had never heard a nurse utter a sharp or impatient word.

Hospital ships were required by international law to be fully lighted, so at night they moved away from the other ships. This way the enemy couldn't use their lights to find the other ships nearby. Throughout the night the hospital ships cruised in circles as doctors and nurses worked frantically to save all the patients they could. In the morning the ships moved in closer to shore to receive more wounded.

Some of the nurses left their ships and followed the troops into battle zones. The Allies landed in North Africa on November 8, 1942. Throughout the gray dawn, nurses waited on ships that shuddered from the repercussions of the flashing guns on shore. When the signal was given, they climbed down ladders that hung over the side and into the small landing craft rising and falling in the huge swells of the ocean waves below. They were told to wait until a wave reached its crest before they jumped so they wouldn't injure themselves.

When they reached land, they rolled up their slacks and waded ashore. They spent that first night on the beach, eating canned rations and drinking water from their canteens. Eventually, some were taken by jeep to a three-story building that had been turned into a hospital. There were wounded men everywhere, some French, some American, some Arab. One American tugged at the hem of Ruth Haskell's slacks and asked for a drink of water. As she lifted his head to let him drink from her canteen, she asked, "Where are you hurt?"

The man gasped. "An American woman! Where did you come from?"

"I'm a nurse," she told him proudly.

The operating room in the North African hospital was extremely primitive. It had a bare table, one light swinging overhead, and an old sink. Sniper fire could be heard throughout the night. When the lights went out, the surgeons continued to operate by flashlight as the nurses administered ether and sterilized instruments on into the next day. When they were relieved by more nurses, they found there was no more drinking water, and no water for washing. They ate cold canned rations and slept fully clothed in case they were needed. The nurses continued to follow the troops across North Africa until the enemy forces surrendered in this area in May, 1943.

Some nurses on the European front were sent to Italy aboard the British hospital ship *Newfoundland*. They were supposed to land one day after the soldiers—September 10, 1943—but that night the ship was bombed, despite the fact that it had huge red crosses painted on its funnels. At 5:00 A.M. the nurses were thrown from their beds by the force of a bomb from a German plane. Six British nurses were killed and three American nurses were wounded. The survivors were picked up in lifeboats by another British ship and taken to North Africa.

It was two weeks before the nurses who were not wounded could make their way back to Italy. There, as American troops fought their way across the Italian countryside, the nurses followed behind. Officers who thought that the women would be too weak to work that close to the battles gained new respect for the nurses as they worked round-the-clock nursing the wounded and dying. The nurses were also wonderful for morale, because the men seemed to think if the nurses could take it, so could they.

On February 7, 1944, German planes bombed the 95th Evacuation Hospital, killing sixteen and wounding sixty-four. Nurses Blanche Sigman, Carrie Sheetz, and Marjorie Morrow were killed instantly.

Burning tents fell on patients. The remaining nurses rushed to knock them away. They gathered the few supplies that were left and continued working until February 10, when they were replaced by a new unit. The new unit was also attacked by German shells, and two nurses, Chief Nurse Glenda Spelhaug and 2nd Lieutenant LaVerne Farquhar, were killed. Three nurses, Mary Roberts, Elaine R. Roe, and Virginia Rourke, received the Silver Star; they were the first women ever to receive this award.

In March 1944, nurses were at Anzio, south of Rome, when one of the most fierce battles of World War II took place. German planes were attacking twenty-four hours a day, but the doctors and nurses worked steadily to transfer the wounded to hospital ships waiting off shore.

On D-Day, June 6, 1944, the Allies launched a massive attack on the Normandy beachhead in France. The first nurses waded ashore with the troops, and worked in mobile field hospitals and hospitals set up in cow pastures, open fields, and along roads only a few miles from the battles. Months later, on October 21, 1944, a nurse stationed in France wrote a letter later published in the *Stars and Stripes,* the official armed services newspaper. She wrote:

> The GIs say we rough it. We in our little tent can't see it. True, we are set up in tents, sleep on cots and are subject to the temperament of the weather. We wade ankle deep in mud, but you have to lie in it. . . . You, the men behind the guns, the men driving our tanks, flying our planes, sailing our ships . . . it's to you we doff our helmets. To every GI wearing the American uniform, for you we have the greatest admiration.
>
> Yes, this time we are handing out the bouquets. After taking care of some of your buddies, seeing them when they are brought in bloody, dirty with earth, mud and grime, . . . seeing them gradually

A Red Cross hospital worker in Italy arrives with supplies for World War II troops

brought back to life and consciousness, to see their lips separate into a grin when they first welcome you! It doesn't amaze us to hear one of them say, "Hiya, Babe," or "Holy mackerel, an American woman!"

Lt. Slanger's letter brought about replies from GIs all over the world. One said:

> We are here because we have to be. You are here merely because you felt you were needed. . . . You could be home, soaking yourselves in a bathtub every day, putting on clean clothes over a clean body and crawling in between clean sheets at night. Instead, you endure whatever hardships you must to be where you can do us most good.

Frances Slanger never saw her letter published in the newspaper and she never read any of the replies. The same day she wrote the letter, she was in her tent wrapping Christmas presents (which had to be mailed far ahead of time). A German shell struck her tent. Lt. Slanger died a half hour later.

CHAPTER SEVEN

"She knew as well as I that she was signing her captivity warrant."

On December 7, 1941, the day the Japanese attacked Pearl Harbor, they also attacked Guam, an island in the Pacific. Five Navy nurses were taken prisoner and sent to a military prison at Zentusji, Japan. They were not released until August, 1942. Six Army nurses were among the twenty-nine people killed when the hospital ship *Comfort,* loaded with wounded from the island of Okinawa, was attacked by a Japanese kamikaze "suicide" plane.

The Japanese also soon attacked the Philippines. Authorities there knew that Manila, the largest Philippine city, would soon be in Japanese hands, so some of the nurses were evacuated. Ten Army nurses escaped to Australia by plane; others escaped by sea in a small ship. Built to carry seventy-five people, that day it carried three hundred seventy-five. A pilot boat guided it out through the mine-infested bay to open sea. Suddenly, the patients began screaming in

Nurses on the island of New Guinea. World War II. 1943

pain. When the nurses removed their bandages, they found them infested with red ants. Twenty-seven days later, the ship arrived in Australia. The nurses laughed when they learned the boat on which they had spent twenty-seven days had been labeled "entirely unseaworthy" by the Australian government.

Those doctors and nurses left behind in the Philippines set up a hospital at a place called Bataan. They cared for their patients on beds set in the middle of a sandy river bed with snakes hanging down from mango trees, and monkeys trying to steal what little food they had. Food soon became so scarce, in fact, that mules, water buffalo, and sometimes monkeys were eaten. Rice was cooked in 50-gallon cans. When the rice was gone, malnutrition became common.

The hospital at Bataan was soon filled to capacity. Only those patients who needed surgery and would take at least three weeks to heal were allowed in. By March, 1942, more than 11,000 patients were waiting to be treated in a hospital that was built for one thousand.

During that spring, the hospitals were bombed constantly. Tin roofs landed up in trees and laundry was scattered over the hills. Windows were broken and glass lay everywhere. Beds were tipped over and patients lay moaning on the ground after each raid. Through it all, the doctors refused to leave their operating tables and the nurses stayed by their side.

At Limay, to the north, the hospital was forced to evacuate because the Japanese were headed that way. Nurses stuffed their belongings into barracks bags and pillowcases, and rode out in ambulances, trucks, private cars, even a garbage truck—anything that moved. They reached the dock at Mariveles on April 9 only to find that their ship had left. Bombs started falling, and they dived for the ditches.

Nurses aides at General Hospital in Manila receive their diplomas

Later that day a steamer arrived to take them to safety. A few minutes after they left, the island was attacked again.

Some of the Americans found safety for a while on Corregidor, a fortified island in Manila Bay. Because of the constant danger from bombs, people on Corregidor lived in long tunnels during the war. It was not easy to get back into the tunnels in time when the bombers came. Finally, they put their trust in a white mongrel dog, whose sharp ears could pick up the sound of a plane long before humans could hear it. He would listen for a minute, head cocked, then head for the tunnel. Everyone followed.

On May 3, 1942, General Jonathan M. Wainwright, the Allied commander, told the nurses to get ready to leave. The Philippines was about to fall to the Japanese. As the nurses gathered their belongings, Wainwright shook hands with each one. They boarded launches and, while Japanese searchlights were sweeping the waters around them, were taken to a submarine. For seventeen days on the sub, thirteen women shared four bunks; they slept in shifts. Finally, they arrived safely in Australia. Only four days after they left, Corregidor was surrendered to the Japanese.

More than fifty nurses had refused to leave Corregidor. Captain Annie Mealer spoke for the nurses when she said she would not leave as long as there was one patient at the hospital. Wainwright later said, "I considered and still consider this a truly great act of heroism. She knew as well as I that she was signing her captivity warrant."

On May 7, 1942, Capt. Mealer and some of her staff were assisting in a difficult operation. When they looked up, there in the door stood a Japanese soldier with his bayonet fixed. They calmly finished the surgery before surrendering.

Many of the nurses taken prisoner from Corregidor were taken to the University of Santo Tomas in Manila. There, some 470 women shared three showers and five toilets. With so many people, men and women, under wartime conditions, there was never enough of anything. The prisoners often had to stand in lines two blocks long to get boiled rice or spinach. On Christmas Day, 1944, as a special treat, the cooks were given enough fat to fry rice, and each prisoner got a double portion of sweet potatoes. Eventually they were reduced to eating dogs, rats, and guinea pigs. Most of the women lost 30 pounds or more. Sixty-year-old Major Maude Davison dropped from 159 pounds to 80. When a Red Cross ship arrived carrying kits with coffee, canned butter, cheese, dried fruits, and other delicacies, each prisoner got one kit. The Japanese took the rest. Toward the end of their captivity, there were three to four deaths every day, mostly from malnutrition.

The women kept busy by making underwear from worn-out outer garments and knitting socks from string and yarn. They organized a forbidden camp newspaper and got their news from a garbage truck driver each day. When possible, they listened to radio broadcasts that included a secret code. The radio announcer would play songs that relayed the news through their titles. For instance, if he played "Midnight in Paris," they knew the Americans had entered Paris. The song played when the Americans returned to the Philippines was "Hail, Hail, the Gang's All Here."

On March 12, 1942, General Douglas MacArthur had left Corregidor on a PT boat as the Philippines fell to the Japanese. "I shall return," he told the Filipinos. On October 20, 1944, he fulfilled that promise and began recapturing the country island by island. Finally, on February 3, 1945, six American bombers flew over Santo Tomas. One of the pilots dropped a note. It read, "Roll out the barrel" from the song lyrics, "Roll out the barrel. We'll have a barrel of fun." The nurses wept with joy. They knew their suffering would soon end. That evening they heard the rumbling of tanks and brief machine gun fire. Soon a tank broke through the inner gate and lumbered toward the main building. Other tanks followed. Two officers walked in front of the lead tank.

"Hello, folks," one of them said. The internees went wild. They seized the American soldiers and carried them through the crowd. Then they sang "God Bless America" and "The Star-Spangled Banner." They were free after two and a half years of imprisonment.

More than sixteen hundred nurses were decorated for their service and bravery in World War II. They received such medals as the Silver Star and Legion of Merit, some of the highest honors available. Five hospital ships and one general hospital used during the war were named after Army nurses who had been killed.

CHAPTER EIGHT

The Real-Life MASH War

When the Korean War broke out in 1950, Captain Viola McConnell was the only Army nurse on duty in Korea. She escorted nearly seven hundred American evacuees, mostly women and children, to Japan aboard a Norwegian freighter that normally carried twelve passengers. After their safe arrival in Japan, Captain McConnell requested to be sent back. She was quickly joined by other nurses who were once again being sent to Asian shores.

At the end of World War II, Korea had been divided into two separate governments—North Korea and South Korea. North Korea was occupied by the Soviet Union; South Korea was occupied by the United States. Then, in 1948, South Korea was placed under the control of the United Nations.

On June 25, 1950, South Korea was attacked by the army of North Korea, which hoped to make it a communist country. The United States and the United Nations acted quickly to come to the aid of

South Korea. Two days after the attack, President Harry S. Truman ordered General Douglas MacArthur, commander of the Far East forces, to send in the navy and air force. At the same time, the U.N. Security Council asked its members to also send military aid to South Korea. The U.N. forces included troops from Australia, Great Britain, France, New Zealand, Colombia, the Philippines, Ethiopia, and Belgium. They came, literally, from every part of the world. Nurses were a part of this aid.

Before American nurses were sent to Korea, they had to attend a special school for eight weeks. There they learned to use field equipment and studied dental and surgical subjects, operating techniques, and hospital administration. They also learned to fire small arms, read maps, and use gas masks while under attack. Their motto became "Always Behind the Soldier."

Most of the nurses sent to Korea were flown in and sometimes found themselves immediately involved in the war as the American planes came in low to avoid YAKS, Russian-built fighters. If they arrived in the rainy season, they experienced muddy and slippery roads, mosquitoes that "could eat you alive," rotting clothes, and rusted equipment. Normally in Korea, the summers are filled with monsoon rains, but during August, 1950, the country was in the midst of a drought, and temperatures reached the hundreds. At one point, the Marines lost more men to the heat than they did to the enemy. Winter brought freezing temperatures and terrible winds.

The nurses were sent to Korea so quickly that it was often a while before their equipment caught up with them. The first mobile medical unit in Korea was the 8054 Evacuation Hospital. It included twelve nurses from Tokyo General Hospital. Proper clothing did not arrive until later, so the nurses wore men's clothing, including shoes, which had to be stuffed with socks to make them fit.

The 8054 Evacuation Hospital personnel found themselves without a hospital building, so, like the Civil War nurses, these nurses set about turning a schoolhouse into a hospital. They scrubbed it from top to bottom and set up five operating tables and two receiving wards, one for litter patients and one for critical cases. They used tin cans to hold their supplies. Since there were no cots, the patients were placed on the floor.

Because the roads were so bad in Korea, trains, which were very primitive, were often used to move the wounded from field hospitals to safer areas. Patients were loaded onto litters and passed through the train windows. The windows had to remain open, so flies and dust came in. When the train went through a tunnel, the nurses would cover the patients' faces with damp clothes to protect them from the foul air inside the tunnel. Panic-stricken refugees clung to the sides of the train as it passed through the war-riddled country-side. There was also the danger that the train might be ambushed and bombed.

Fortunately, less than five months after the war began, the U.S. government sent over new hospital trains. The nurses had eight new trains complete with kitchen cars that had hot food and running water. Beds were also provided.

Since the Korean War was a cooperative effort of the United Nations, American nurses worked side by side with nurses from other countries. Denmark had sent a medical team and a hospital ship, Italy organized a Red Cross hospital, Sweden ran one field hospital, and Norway sent a mobile surgical hospital.

Hospitals during wartime often have to be mobile. This is why, during the Korean War, a new type of combat hospital called a Mobile Army Surgical Hospital (MASH) was invented. MASH units, made famous by the popular TV series, were located as close to the front as possible. These units were so portable, doctors, nurses, and patients were able to move at a moment's notice.

Often, a warning came over the loudspeaker: "Attention all personnel. Take cover. The base is under rocket attack. Security alert. Condition red." Sirens wailed, the ground shook, the air was filled with bright lights and sounds of battle. Hospital personnel dove for cover.

When the enemy got too close, the nurses and doctors prepared to "bug out" (move). They needed only half an hour to get the patients ready to be loaded onto helicopters. Bed patients were strapped onto litters and the wounded able to walk were on stand-by, ready to go. A whole hospital could be evacuated in two hours. Some nurses and doctors would stay behind with patients who were too critical to be moved. They often found themselves without electricity because the generator had been hit, or without water because the water tank had been destroyed. They might even have to fight for their lives if the enemy overran the camp.

It was important to practice setting up and taking down expandables (metal boxes that when put together became labs, operating rooms, or X-ray facilities). Units called inflatables could be made into receiving areas, post-op wards, or holding units. When inflated, they looked like huge space modules glued together. Often the units were placed in what was called a surgical-T shape. This meant there were six operating cubicles, three on each side of an open hallway and divided from each other by tall cabinets.

Some of the MASH units were run, not by army medical staff, but by medical volunteers. The Norwegian MASH unit consisted of volunteers who were supposed to be in Korea for six months. But of the 632 Norwegians who served with MASH, over 100 stayed on voluntarily for more than a year. There were a total of 111 female nurses in this unit, including some American and Korean nurses.

MASH units needed every nurse they could find. They often worked to the point of exhaustion. It was not uncommon to handle as many as 50 to 60 casualties in an hour. In 1953, NorMASH, the Norwegian unit, performed 173 operations in a 72-hour period.

Some nurses were assigned to Korean civilian hospitals. They found conditions there quite different from those in their own countries. For instance, in Korea, it was the custom to toss water over things to be cleaned and leave them to be air-dried. When it came to cleaning hospital floors, this meant the floors rotted quickly or in winter became sheets of ice that children would slide on.

It was also the custom in Korean hospitals to place the patients on the floor and for patients to be accompanied by as many relatives as possible. People lined the corridors, stairs, and wards. There were few hospital rules, so it was not uncommon to see people peering through a crack in the operating room door to watch surgery. Since the hospitals could not provide food for patients, families brought in their own raw fish, onions, sacks of rice, and jars of pickled vegetables that they cooked on little charcoal stoves in the corridors.

The nurses learned that Koreans had different standards of cleanliness from their own. Because Korea was such a poor country, many patients had never seen soap. One nurse found a patient whose feet had not been washed in three years. In one Seoul hospital, eight hundred soldiers were lying on six hundred dirty army cots, some sleeping head to foot, two in one bed. Patients with contagious diseases were in the same room with the other patients.

Since Korean nurses had little training, the American nurses were supposed to help them learn about sanitation and hospital procedure. The language barrier made this difficult, but eventually they learned to work together.

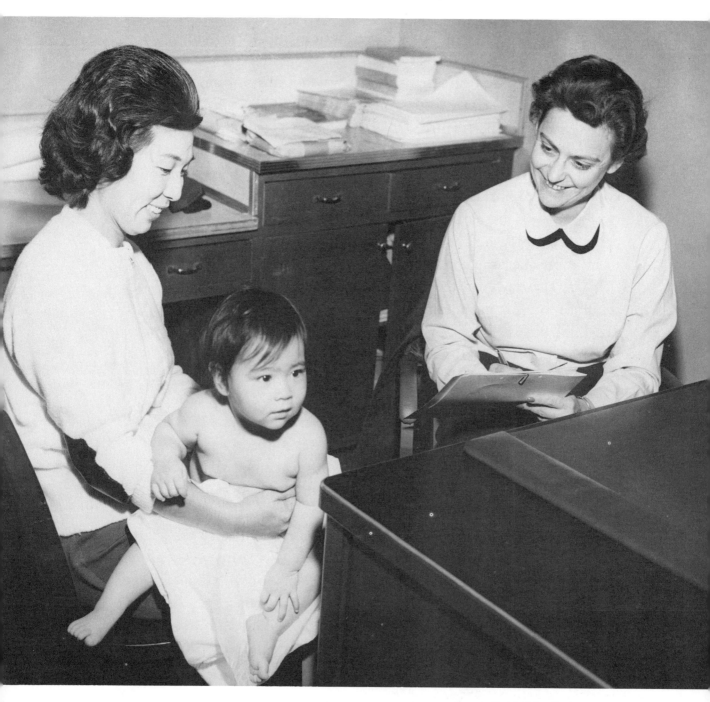

Army Health Nurse in Korea counsels Korean mother in the Well Child Clinic, 1964

On June 23, 1951, the Soviet Union proposed cease-fire negotiations. The truce talks lasted more than two years. Finally, on July 27, 1953, the truce agreement was signed at Panmunjom. The war that had left Korea in shambles and killed 1.5 million U.N. and communist soldiers was at an end. Once more, the nurses packed their duffle bags and headed for home. Major General Raymond W. Bliss, surgeon general, said of the war nurses in Korea, "You have never seen anything like it. Conditions were awful, yet the nurses wrought miracles overnight. They are heroic women."

CHAPTER NINE

The Vietnam War Begins

The United States had barely recovered from the Korean War when troops began shipping out for Vietnam in 1962. By then, the French had been fighting the communists in French Indochina (now called Vietnam) for eighteen years. Early on, the U.S. had given the French money for the war and had provided American military "advisers" to help fight the Vietcong. But by 1964 over fifteen thousand American troops were serving there.

Greater United States' involvement came about when the United States destroyer *Maddox* was attacked by three North Vietnamese PT boats in the Gulf of Tonkin. President Lyndon Johnson ordered air strikes against North Vietnamese bases. By May 1965, fifty thousand U.S. troops were in Vietnam.

During the fighting in Vietnam, the French had done little in the way of providing hospitals. At the famous Battle of Dien Bien Phu in March of 1953, for instance, the French had expected to fly the wounded out of the country, and had built a hospital with only forty-four beds. As hundreds of casualties came pouring in, only a handful of doctors and medics were there to care for them. The only nurse was Lieutenant Genevieve de Galard-Terraube. She had flown in with a hospital plane and had planned to fly out with a load of casualties. But the plane had been damaged by shell fire. Lieutenant de Galard-Terraube remained on duty and became known as "The Angel of Dien Bien Phu."

The U.S. Army opened its first hospital in Nha Trang in 1962 and the U.S. Navy opened a hospital in Saigon that same year. In addition, two navy hospital ships, the *Repose* and the *Sanctuary,* were stationed off the coast of Vietnam. The air force also built a hospital in Cam Ranh Bay and began operating air evacuation units that could transport patients from Vietnam hospitals to other hospitals outside the war area. By 1969, there were twenty-six hospitals in operation.

The hospitals desperately needed nurses, so the U.S. government began recruiting American nurses to go to Vietnam. The Vietnam war nurses came from a wide variety of backgrounds. Some came from rich families, some from poor. Some were widely traveled; others had never been out of their hometown. Many signed contracts to enter one of the branches of the armed services while still in nursing school. Others were veterans who had been in nursing for many years.

All the new nurses would have one thing in common, however—basic training. Basic training for Vietnam nurses was intense. They were often up at 2:30 A.M. for the 4 A.M. formation, where they learned how to march and how to crawl along the ground. They practiced avoiding trip wires, punji pits—holes filled with sharp stakes—and other kinds of booby traps in mock Vietnamese villages.

Wounded servicemen on stretchers on the deck of hospital ship USS Sanctuary

They learned how to carry pounds of gear—mess kits, helmets, gas masks, sleeping bags, canteens, shovels, and heavy canvas tents— while marching. They carried M-16 rifles and 45-caliber pistols and learned to read maps. They learned how to perform emergency tracheotomies on anesthetized goats. This procedure of inserting a breathing tube in the throat of a patient who was choking on blood saved many lives.

In order to teach the nurses how to work under the pressure of a MAS-CAL situation (mass casualties), men acting as wounded patients had tags tied on their bodies saying what was wrong with them. The nurses had to decide whether to send them right to the operating room, set them aside for surgery, or, if they were beyond hope, give them painkillers to ease their suffering. (This system of sorting out patients and treating those who might best benefit is called "triage.") If nurses were not able to make these decisions quickly, many more patients would die.

Before being sent overseas, American nurses first had to spend time in U.S. hospitals, where they would be given further training in more specialized work. They might become circulating nurses, who stay outside the operating room organizing which patients would go into surgery next. Or they might train as scrub nurses, who assist the surgeon inside the operating room.

Air Force nurses received special training. They had to learn how to carry out their duties while flying 550 miles an hour at an altitude of thirty-five thousand feet. They were given practice runs in a mock-up flight before they were sent on real flights. They also learned how to leave a ditched plane at sea by practicing in special water-survival tanks.

After this specialized training, the nurses were ready to be shipped to Vietnam. After a very long flight, with stops in Hawaii and the

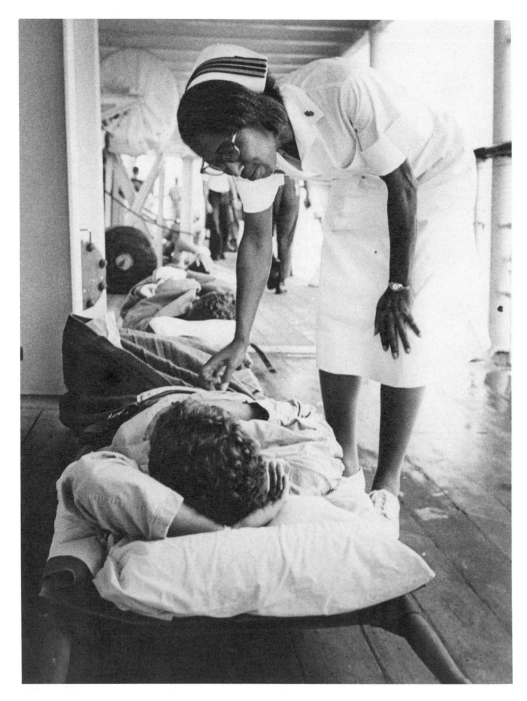

Navy nurse with patient aboard hospital ship USS Repose

Hospital corpsman and nurse discuss a patient's condition aboard the hospital ship USS Repose

Philippines, the American nurses would arrive in Vietnam. The nurses' first view was miles of runways and tin-roofed hangars. After whizzing past hundreds of helicopters lined up in rows, their blades folded up like wings of sleeping bats, the nurses were welcomed by heat waves bouncing off the runways if it were summer; bone-freezing temperatures if it were winter.

The newly arrived U.S. nurses found life in this tiny country much different from what they had known back home. Because of the French influence, city streets had French names. Louvered windows like those in New Orleans lined the wide, tree-lined streets. Billboards had advertisements in English, French, and Vietnamese so as not to miss any possible customers.

Scattered amidst the classic French architecture were supply sheds, ammunition dumps, repair shops, motor pools, barracks, and mess halls, all painted military green. Sandbags were placed on sheet metal roofs to hold them down during typhoons or mortar attacks, and sandbagged trenches zigzagged around buildings.

Life in the Vietnam countryside differed greatly from that of the city. Here, a village consisted of several hamlets separated by paddy fields. Each hamlet had a chief and each village had a council made up of chiefs from the hamlets.

Instead of brick or wood houses, there were huts made of bamboo, straw, and mud. Roofs were made of thatched palm leaves and the floors were packed-down earth. Water buffalo and oxen grazed in rice paddies that lined the highways. In areas near the sea, goats, skinny pigs, and scrawny chickens dozed underneath stilt huts while fishermen nearby pulled in their catch with nets. Thick, lush forests of bamboo hid elephants, tigers, deer, panthers, and bears.

The cities were filled with different dangers. Hotels and embassies were ripped apart by explosive charges; bombs and rockets reduced whole neighborhoods to rubble. Sometimes the only businesses open were the coffin makers. Running battles with gunfire took place on the golf course, and churches were turned into shambles.

Instead of the modern, air-conditioned stores of the United States, the nurses had to get used to streets lined with vendors selling everything from oil paintings to refrigerators. Dead animals hung in doorways in a land where shopping for dinner is done each day.

Almost everyone in this country dressed alike. Women wore *ao dai,* a long flowing dress that reached the ankles but was split up the side to the waist. *Quans,* long white trousers, were worn underneath.

Saigon street scene

Men were either in camouflage fatigues and boots, or black pajamas and wooden clogs or bare feet. Both men and women in the countryside wore black pajamas and conical woven bamboo hats as they tended the animals or worked in the rice paddies.

Like Korea, Vietnam was a very poor country, so the nurses knew that hospitals would not be big, modern structures like the ones found in most U.S. cities. They also knew from their studies in nursing history that wartime hospitals were usually primitive and makeshift. In Vietnam, some hospitals were in ramshackle wooden buildings or metal Quonset huts sometimes so dirty that the nurses had to sweep out inches of trash before the bunks and lavatories could be put in place. Other hospitals might simply be the MASH units, first used in the Korean War.

Because hospitals could be attacked at any time, the hospital compounds were often surrounded by radar screens and soldiers in guard towers. Tanks rolled across the compounds, and the sound of rifles, mortars, and artillery was always present. Coiled barbed wire was everywhere. The boonies (foliage) that surrounded the compounds were so thick that the Vietcong could be hiding there at any time, watching and waiting.

When the first hospital units arrived by ship, the nurses lived and worked in tents while the hospitals were being built. Later, nurses lived in Quonset huts, rough buildings, or MUST tents. (MUST stands for Medical Unit, Self-Contained, Transportation). MUST units could also be used as medical and surgical wards. Smaller units were attached to a main building that housed the operating rooms. Inside the operating room were floor-to-ceiling shelves filled with bandages, first-aid supplies, and IVs.

The quarters were often surrounded by sandbags as protection against rockets and red dust that seemed to seep in everywhere. The

Navy nurses in their quarters at U.S. Naval Support Activity Hospital

nurses fought a losing battle trying to keep their areas clean. Often, just when they thought they had things under control, a fleet of choppers (helicopters) would come along and the red dust would take over again. If that weren't enough, there was the constant attack of mosquitoes and rats to contend with.

The nurses learned there were two seasons in Vietnam—the dry season from November to February when the weather was often pleasant, and the rainy season from late May to October. In between, during March, April and parts of May, the air was so humid, the nurses were constantly wet. During the rainy season, rain would pour down so hard it was impossible to see more than five feet ahead. High winds and gusts blew the water everywhere. The red dust would turn to mud, seeping into the operating room and through the walls and floors of the living quarters.

Some nurses tried to fix up their primitive quarters by scrounging for materials or ordering paint and curtains from catalogs. Others bought household items from local merchants.

The nurses were often without the simplest items that women in the United States take for granted such as shampoo, perfume, and other toiletries. Water for bathing might or might not be hot or even warm and could not be used even for brushing teeth, since it was unsafe to drink. The Vietnamese used polluted water from irrigation ditches, canals, streams, or shallow pools. These same waters were used for bathing, laundry, and for washing their animals.

Nurses knew that war can create great hardship as far as food is concerned. But Vietnam nurses did have plenty of one item—rice. Rice is the most popular crop in Vietnam, and the people there often eat rice three times a day. The nurses also ate strange fresh fruits like mangosteens, which taste like a cross between a peach and a pineapple, and water-buffalo stew or water-buffalo burgers along with their

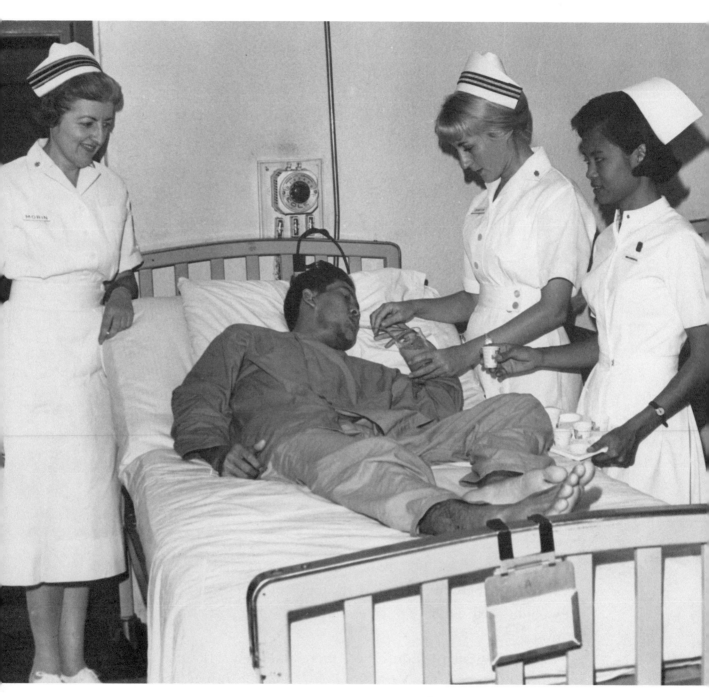

Nurses at Saigon Navy Hospital attend a Vietnamese casualty

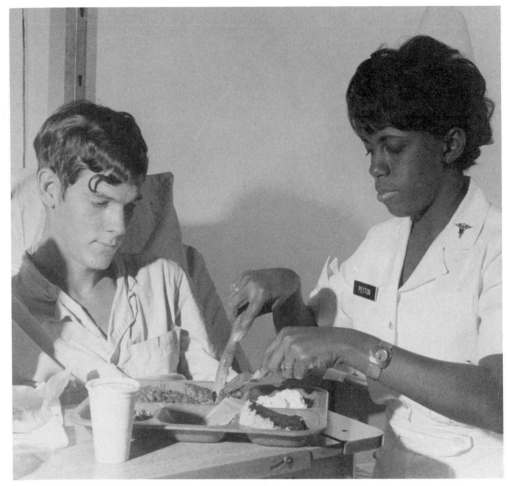

Army nurse at Field Hospital cuts food for serviceman

army chow or c-rations. Not long after they arrived, they began dreaming of their first "R and R" (rest and recreation) leave when they could go to Hong Kong for a hot shower and an American-type hamburger or steak.

Nurses in Vietnam found there were still men who resented their presence and made life hard for them. On the other hand, just as some Civil War doctors had been thankful for their nurses' help, many Army doctors in "Nam" felt the nurses were invaluable. And once the casualties started pouring in, bad housing, water, food, and petty grievances were forgotten. The nurses thought only of the real reason they were there—to take care of the wounded and dying.

CHAPTER TEN

The War of the Helicopters

Vietnam became known as the war of the helicopters. Instead of being strapped onto litters and placed on trucks or trains, the wounded were strapped onto litters and placed in helicopters. Because of these fast-moving "ambulances," the recovery rate for the patients was estimated to be 98.4 percent, the best ever.

The helicopters that rescued the wounded were often kept right outside the hospital door, ready to go at a moment's notice, so the nurses in Vietnam became used to the constant noise of the "dust-offs." (The helicopters were called "dust-offs" because of the dust they raised when they came and went.) After the helicopters made the short trips to the field hospitals, jets would be used to transport the patients home after surgery or treatment.

The Air Evac system itself was not new. In February 1943, during World War II, the first class of Army Nurse Corps flight nurses graduated from the School of Air Evacuation in Kentucky. In December, two Navy nurses were given air evacuation training. Then they were sent to Rio de Janeiro to help set up an air evacuation training program for the Brazilian Air Force nurses.

In 1944, the first naval school of air evacuation for casualties was opened at the Naval Air Station in Alameda, California. Twenty-four nurses were given instruction and a base hospital was opened on the island of Guam. There, nurses stood by for the air evacuation of casualties from Iwo Jima and Okinawa.

The Air Evac flight preparations in Vietnam typically began around 4:30 A.M. The nurses would leave their trailers dressed in flight uniforms of caps, blouses, slacks, and flight jackets. Some carried guns and rifles. After eating, they got a short briefing about what kind of cases they would be handling. Then the nurses boarded the camouflaged aircraft, usually a four-engine jet that carried cargo into Vietnam and the wounded out. They usually left around 7:00 A.M.

Once inside the plane, the nurses were in charge until they reached their destination. They could order the pilots to turn back, to fly at different altitudes, or even to make unscheduled landings. Each flight was different, depending on the type of patients on board. For example, the nurses had to decide whether to risk landing in a field with a short runway where the plane might have to brake suddenly if the plane carried a patient who was hemorrhaging and would be harmed by this abrupt movement.

While in the air, the nurses gave out medicine, took temperatures, changed dressings and sheets, rubbed backs, passed out meals, fed patients, and attended to the medical needs of each patient. They joked that they "walked" across the Pacific Ocean because they were constantly on their feet.

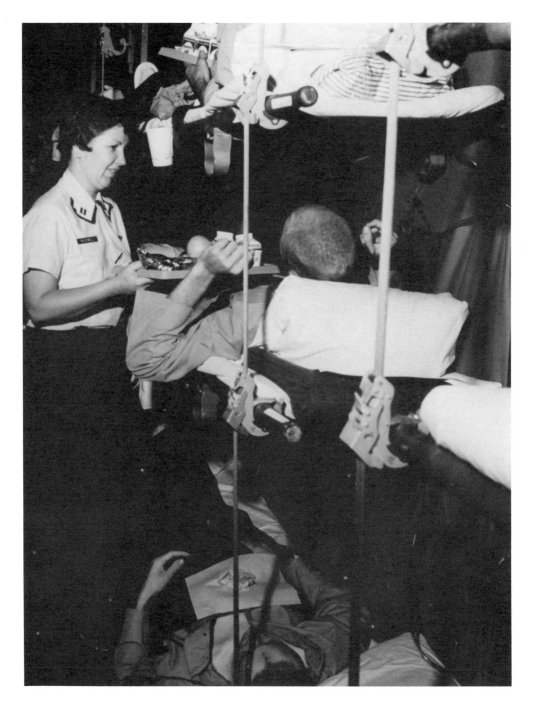

On board aircraft evacuating wounded servicemen from Vietnam to Japan

Most flights were routine. The patients were very happy to be going home. But sometimes there was a problem with patients suffering battle fatigue. One patient grabbed a fire ax during a flight and tried to chop his way out. Another time a patient kept insisting there were people standing on the wings of the plane, which was thirty thousand feet up in the air.

The pilots were always very careful to fly as smoothly as possible. When the plane set down in the States, it was met by a fire truck because the airport personnel knew the patients would not be able to help themselves if there was a fire on landing. Ambulances also pulled up alongside the plane, and medics would transfer the patients to the hospital.

Back in Vietnam, the choppers would be bringing in their bloody loads from the battlefields. At the announcement of "Incoming Wounded," the nurses in the hospital compound would rush to get into their fatigues, flak jackets, and helmets. They raced to the hospital as the sound of the choppers grew louder. As the helicopters came in over the mountains or tree tops, the nurses grabbed the gurneys from the emergency room and rushed outside. As soon as the casualties were unloaded, the "dust-off" was back in the air, on its way to pick up more.

Suddenly the emergency room would be chaos, filled with shouts, screams, and moans. The floors were covered with blood. The wounded were so packed in, there was hardly room for the nurses to move. More wounded arrived every minute and dead bodies in bags were lined up outside the doors, waiting to be taken to the morgue.

"We need more plasma," a nurse would call.

"Get an IV over here," a doctor would shout.

The nurses began cutting the soldiers' uniforms away so they could see the wounds better. Each patient was hooked up to an IV bottle containing life-saving fluids; each received a shot of morphine for pain. Comforting hands and words of reassurance were given to the wounded.

Among the most painful wounds were those caused by Bouncing Betties, land-mine explosive charges that bounced up to waist level before exploding. Because the risk of infection was so great, doctors would often first just stop the bleeding, remove the metal fragments or bullets, clean the wound, and cover it with sterile gauze. When they were sure the wound was not infected, they would close the wound.

When the nurses left the operating room after mass casualties, their scrubs would be covered with blood, the clothes underneath would be covered with blood, even their bodies were covered with blood. As they walked through the wards, their boots left bloody footprints behind. Many nurses worked twelve-hour shifts, seven days a week.

In addition to the American Armed Services nurses on duty in Vietnam, there were also Red Cross workers and civilian nurses from Germany, France, and the United States. They worked in hospitals even more primitive than the ones built by the American military. Some of these hospitals had been built by the French in the 1800s, and much of their equipment looked just as old. Vietnam, a poor country, was unable to afford new, modern equipment. One Saigon hospital had an X-ray machine that was 40 years old. The nurses learned to improvise with supplies. Cots were used as hospital beds, but even then there might be two or more patients to a bed. Plastic bags were filled with sand to become weights for broken bones. Whatever was handy was put to use.

Civilian nurses lived under just as dangerous conditions as military nurses, sometimes even more so since they were there "on their own." In April 1969, for instance, a group of German nurses, aged nineteen to twenty-eight, climbed into a jeep for a Sunday outing. All five, three women and two men, had been working in hospitals run by the Aid Service of Malta, a Catholic organization. They were captured by the North Vietnamese and only two of them, Monika Schwinn and Bernhard Diehl, survived the four years of captivity.

The nurses in Vietnam also cared for civilian war casualties, especially children who had lost eyes, arms, or legs. In addition to nursing these victims, the Vietnam Refugee program was set up by American medical personnel to take medicine each day to Vietnamese refugee camps. "Operation Cleft Lip" was organized by the U.S. Marines. They arranged for surgery that would correct facial deformities of children in the country.

Many Vietnamese were very superstitious. They believed illnesses were caused by sorcerers who had something of the sick person—a photograph, a lock of hair, a piece of clothing. People sometimes refused to go to the hospital because they believed if they left their village they would lose contact with their ancestors and spirits and would get worse. Instead of medicine, they used charms, sacrifices, and prayers. They set off firecrackers to frighten the shy spirits, offered imitation paper money to the greedy spirits, and were polite to the angry ones.

Some American nurses visited a leper colony located in an isolated valley between mountains and the South China Sea. It was run by French nuns and was a peaceful place, because the Vietcong were afraid to go there. American nurses and doctors helped the nuns by treating some of the residents, many of whom had deformed faces, missing fingers and toes, and were often blind.

Most American nurses were sent to Vietnam for one year. During that year, they suffered terrible stress. They were in constant danger. Most counted the days when their tour of duty would be over and they would be back "stateside."

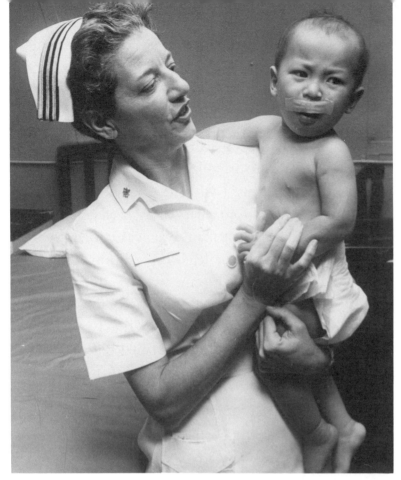

Navy nurse
with small
Vietnamese
patient
at Da Nang,
Vietnam

Army nurse
removes stitches
after eye operation
on Vietnamese
orphan

90

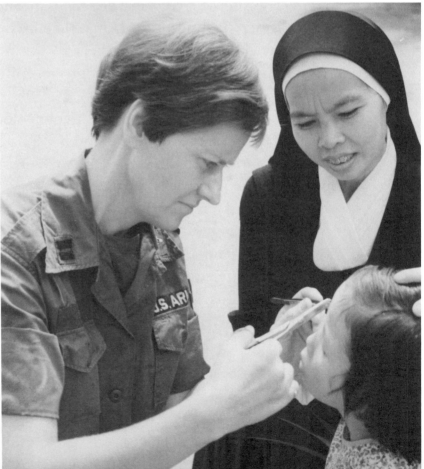

Navy nurses during farewell ceremony aboard USS Repose

CHAPTER ELEVEN

The End of War?

In 1973, a cease-fire agreement was signed in Paris. Over fifty-six thousand men and women had been killed and three hundred thousand wounded in the Vietnam War. One thousand two hundred men were missing in action. In Vietnam, those who were able began celebrating and planning for their return to the United States. Some nurses were left behind to care for the troops wounded while "cleaning up" and to help with the civilian victims of the war—the refugees and thousands of orphans.

As in other wars, American nurses were among the Vietnam casualties. The first Army nurse killed was First Lieutenant Sharon Lane, a twenty-six-year-old woman from Canton, Ohio, who died when a rocket exploded next to her hut on June 8, 1969. Other nurses died in helicopter crashes and many were wounded by rocket or sapper attacks. (Sappers were specially trained enemy soldiers who infiltrated the bases.)

As the Vietnam nurses' DEROS (Date of Expected Return from Overseas) approached, the "short-timers" began thinking of hot water, flushing toilets, telephones, refrigerators, shopping, and "real" food—hamburgers, milk, and ice cream. As they boarded the "Freedom Bird" to go home, they worried that the plane might be shot down or something else might keep them from making it home.

In fact, the last nurse to die in Vietnam, Capt. Mary Therese Klinker, was killed in a plane crash while evacuating Vietnamese orphans from Saigon in 1975. The Americans evacuated as many Vietnamese as possible from the country to begin a new life in the United States. Among the evacuees were two thousand orphans who would be adopted by families in the United States. On April 4th, a military transport plane took off from Vietnam carrying 226 orphans as part of "Operation Babylift." On board were seventy-seven Americans who had volunteered to escort the children to the United States.

Fifteen minutes after takeoff, the doors blew off and oxygen masks dropped down. The volunteers ran up and down the aisles switching the masks from child to child so they could breathe. The pilot turned back and crash-landed in a rice paddy near Saigon. Seventy-five orphans and fifty Americans were killed in the crash.

After returning home, many nurses suffered PTSD (post-traumatic stress disorders)—nightmares, anxiety, sweating. Some told stories of how they rushed out of their houses when they heard the sound of a helicopter, or threw themselves under their beds when they heard a loud noise.

But the people back home did not want to hear about the horrible things the nurses had seen or heard in Vietnam, and the nurses were angry at not being able to express themselves. They had learned to "shut down" their feelings while in Vietnam and continued to do this after they came home. Many refused to seek treatment because they felt that asking for help was a sign of weakness. Vietnam nurses didn't cry. If they did, they might never stop.

Here at home, many had the same feelings of hopelessness and helplessness they had experienced in Vietnam when they put men back together and sent them home to a life as paraplegics or amputees. When they encountered a Vietnam veteran back home they wondered, "Does he hate me?"

They should have been able to receive help for these psychological problems at some of the veteran facilities throughout the United States, but the facilities were often set up for men only, and not for taking care of women, who were, after all, in the minority. Male counselors were not as understanding of the special problems of women. The women were made to feel they were not "real veterans." The Veterans of Foreign Wars, and Vietnam Veterans Against the War rejected them as members. One nurse recalled walking into the Veterans Administration only to be asked by the person at the desk, "Where's the veteran?"

The nurses were angry and decided to do something about it. In 1978, Lynda Van Devanter formed the Women's Project of the Vietnam Veterans of America. This association formed a network to help Vietnam nurses. Counseling groups were organized. They also fought for better veterans' benefits.

In 1983, the nurses convinced the Veterans Administration to establish an Advisory Committee on Women Veterans. Medical centers appointed coordinators for women's medical and psychological aid. Over 3,000 women veterans were surveyed to find out about the effects of Agent Orange, a chemical used to kill the vegetation in

Vietnam that veterans say has caused grave health problems for them.

In 1969, Vietnam nurse Diane Evans returned to the United States, and, like many others, had trouble readjusting to civilian life.

"My reality was Vietnam," she says. "I had lost touch with everyone back home—friends, relatives, family. They couldn't understand why I was so different, why I just couldn't be my happy old self again. They really had no comprehension of what I or the other veterans had been through."

Diane could only take three months of civilian life before she reenlisted in the Army. She was stationed at Fort Sam Houston in Texas, married, and started a family, but she still couldn't get the Vietnam experience out of her mind. In 1982, she went to Washington, D.C., for the dedication of the Vietnam Veterans Memorial. "In thirteen years I hadn't cried," she said. "Now my tears were uncontrollable."

Diane got counseling for her problems, and back in Minnesota where she lived she attended a state salute to Vietnam veterans—the only woman to attend. Artwork was included as part of the salute, and she asked one sculptor, a Vietnam veteran himself, if he had ever thought of sculpting a Vietnam nurse. Roger Brodin sculpted a seven-foot statue of a nurse carrying the helmet of a soldier. When he showed it to Diane, she knew it belonged at the Vietnam Wall.

In 1984, the Vietnam Women's Memorial Project was founded. The purpose of the memorial is not only to honor the nurses who served in Vietnam, but all non-combat women and men who were there.

Among the hundreds of names on the Vietnam Veterans Memorial are ten nurses—eight women and two men. Not only are their names engraved on this very important memorial, but they have memorials named for them across the United States. They are:

2ND LT. CAROL ANN DRAZBA

In 1965, Lt. Drazba volunteered to go to Vietnam. She was stationed at the 3rd Field Hospital near Saigon and was on her way for a weekend of rest when the helicopter she, Elizabeth Ann Jones (another nurse), and five other people were traveling in, crashed. The high school in her hometown of Dunmore, Pennsylvania, established a living memorial to Carol. Each year a $300 award is given to a student seeking a career in the health-care field.

2ND LT. ELIZABETH ANN JONES

Lt. Jones was also assigned to the 3rd Field Hospital near Saigon and was aboard the helicopter that killed Lt. Drazba. Elizabeth was engaged to Lt. Col. Charles M. Honour, Jr., the pilot of the helicopter that crashed.

1ST LT. HEDWIG DIANE ORLOWSKI

Lt. Orlowski had been in Vietnam almost one year with the 67th Evacuation Hospital in Qui Nhon. She was on temporary assignment to Pleiku to assist with the wounded when the C-47 transport plane she was on crashed on the way back to Qui Nhon.

CAPT. ELEANOR GRACE ALEXANDER

Capt. Alexander was on the same plane from Pleiku that killed Hedwig Orlowski. Eleanor had asked to be assigned to Vietnam and was stationed at the 85th Field Evacuation Hospital, also at Qui Nhon. Her hometown of Rivervale, New Jersey, has dedicated a park in her honor.

1ST LT. KENNETH R. SHOEMAKER, JR.

Although definitely in the minority and usually known as medics in the Armed Forces, men have also been a part of the nursing profession since the famous poet, Walt Whitman, signed on as a nurse during the Civil War. Lt. Shoemaker, who also died on the plane from Pleiku, joined the Army Nurse Corps in 1966 after graduation from St. Joseph's Hospital School of Anesthesia in Lancaster, Pennsylvania. He was also assigned to the 67th Evacuation Hospital at Qui Nhon.

1ST LT. JEROME EDWIN OLMSTED

The fourth nurse who died in the transport plane crash at Qui Nhon, Lt. Olmsted was a nurse anesthetist with Lt. Shoemaker in the 67th Evacuation Hospital. He had joined the Army Nurse Corps in 1966, shortly after becoming a father.

2ND LT. PAMELA DOROTHY DONOVAN

Born in Ireland, 2nd Lt. Donovan grew up in Boston and was assigned to the 85th Field Evacuation Hospital in Qui Nhon and had been there only three months when she became seriously ill and died. A road leading to St. Gabriel's Monastery in Brighton, Massachusetts, was named in her honor in 1969.

LT. COL. ANNIE RUTH GRAHAM

Lt. Col. Graham was a career Army nurse who had served in Europe during the Second World War. She left active duty in 1945, but returned during the Korean War. In November 1967, she was assigned as chief nurse, 91st Evacuation Hospital in Tuy Hoa, Vietnam. She suffered a hemorrhage while on duty and died in Japan where she had been sent for emergency surgery.

1ST LT. SHARON ANN LANE

Lt. Lane was the only nurse who died under enemy attack in Vietnam. The Aultman Hospital School of Nursing in Canton, Ohio, named a women's health center after its former employee, and Fitzsimmons Army Medical Center, where she was also stationed, dedicated the Lane Recovery Suite in her honor. The Vietnam Veterans of America, Chapter 199, in Canton, Ohio, dedicated their chapter to her and started a nursing scholarship in her name. Stark County, Ohio, erected a statue of Lt. Lane to honor the men and women who served in Vietnam.

CAPT. MARY THERESE KLINKER

Capt. Klinker was the last nurse and only U.S. Air Force Nurse Corps member to be killed in Vietnam. She cared for the wounded men being sent from Vietnam to hospitals in Japan, the Philippines, Hawaii, and the United States. She was assigned at Clarke Air Force Base in the Philippines when she volunteered to help airlift the orphans out of Saigon. The McDonnell Douglas Corporation sponsors an annual "Mary T. Klinker Flight Nurse of the Year Award" which is given to the Air Force nurse who has made a significant contribution in nursing.

Finally, the Vietnam nurses made history in 1987 when one of them was elected head of a national veteran's group. Former army nurse Mary Stout was elected president of the Vietnam Veterans of America, the first woman to lead a national veterans' organization. She received more than 60 percent of the votes cast by about 400 delegates, defeating two male combat vets who ran against her. One veteran, when asked about his feelings about having a woman president, said, "To me, she is a vet. She served in Vietnam just like the rest of us."

Today, ex-Vietnam nurses may be found working in civilian and military hospitals throughout the world. Because they were used to high-tension jobs in Vietnam, many have taken jobs in intensive care units or emergency rooms. They have often had problems adjusting to their new peacetime jobs. Some have become workaholics; others feel their jobs are meaningless after Vietnam. When people ask them how they managed to survive under the intense conditions of war, they often answer simply, "We had to." One nurse probably spoke for war nurses of all time when she said:

It's taken years for many of us to be able to appreciate the positive aspects of it. So many times we remember the most seriously wounded patients who were evacuated, so we never knew what happened to them, or the ones who died. We did so much that too often we wonder if we could have done more, rather than remembering all the lives that were saved and the people who got home. It wasn't easy, it wasn't pleasant, and it certainly wasn't glamorous. We had a job to do, and we did it well.

Index